C0-DAN-486

Sugar Gliders
A Comprehensive Guide To
Pocket Pets

David Oconner

ISBN-13: 978-1478263906

Table of Contents

David Oconner

What Are Sugar Gliders?

Sugar gliders are small marsupials that are indigenous to Australia, Tasmania, New Guinea, and several other islands around Indonesia. While sugar gliders are now kept as pets and are domesticated, in the wild, sugar gliders dwell in trees and are found in groups of up to 30. In their native tree-dwelling environment, sugar gliders feed on insects and small vertebrates, as well as the sap of various species of trees like the eucalyptus, acacia, and gum tree. Their habit of feeding on both sap from plant life, as well as insects and the flesh of small vertebrates makes the sugar glider an omnivorous, instead of an herbivore, which is often assumed of the small creature.

Their diet also fits well into their habitat because all of their dietary needs can be met by the trees around them. Additionally, sugar gliders are equipped with a specialized anatomy that makes living in the tree tops a breeze for them. Sugar gliders are equipped with spreads of extra skin that extends from the body to the legs and arms of the sugar glider. This transforms their body into a sort of kite-like shape, allowing for easy gliding from one area to another. This spread of skin is actually known as the patagium, and is classified as a thin membrane.

The patagium, as well as the sugar gliders love for sweet sap is how the little marsupials got their name, and is also an easy way to remember some quick and important facts about the sugar glider.

In addition to having the ability to glide through the air, the sugar glider has the ability to steer his general direction by using their tails as rudders. Their tails are relatively long, allowing for excellent navigation for the 50 meters they are capable of staying in the air.

Other anatomically unique qualities the sugar glider has are opposable fingers and toes. Each front foot has five different fingers, each with sharp claws attached. These sharp claws allow the glider to attach onto a number of surfaces. In the wild, this can mean tree surfaces to prevent from falling. In captivity, gliders may attach to their owners and other surfaces in the house when out to play.

The back feet have one large opposable toe, two toes that are fused together but each have separate claws. This particular section of the sugar glider's foot is used specifically for grooming.

The sugar glider also has very large eyes, which lend themselves well to seeing in the dark. This is perfect since sugar gliders are nocturnal in nature. Thus, their eyes put them at a great advantage in the dark. Also an advantage to them, is the position of their eyes, which is set widely near the sides of the head. This allows the sugar glider to have a wide range of view by which to keep a watch out for predators. This is an extremely important feature since sugar gliders are so small.

The average glider measures around six inches in length, which doesn't include their lengthy tail which can be just as long as their body. At adulthood, the sugar glider weighs around 4-6 ounces (depending on gender – with males being larger than the female).

Sugar gliders have extremely thick fur that is also very soft. This fur is grey with a black stripe running down the length of the body. This cute little stripe lines up perfectly with the spine, starting at the head and finishing off at the tail that is generally tipped completely in black as though it has been dipped in black ink. Sugar gliders also have black markings that appear on the legs, face, and back.

Although sugar gliders are small pets, they have a very sizable lifespan. Most people assume that all small pets have a short lifespan, but sugar gliders may live from 12 to 15 years when cared for properly. This includes providing the glider with the right company, diet, and care, all to be discussed in further detail later.

What Are Marsupials?

Marsupials are a classification of animals defined by the unique manner in which the young are born. Marsupials are best known for raising their young in pouch, but few people realize why exactly this is done.

Marsupial babies are born in a highly immature state, unlike mammal babies that are delivered at a time when they are able to survive outside of the womb. Because of the birth of an underdeveloped baby, marsupial babies then continue to develop outside the mother's womb, and attached to the mother's nipple. In many cases, the mother has a pouch in which the baby is housed until they are more fully developed and ready to be exposed to the world outside. Sugar gliders have this pouch, and thus the mother glider raises the babies there for up to two and a half months after the babies are born.

Aside from sugar gliders, other marsupials include kangaroos, koalas, opossums, wombats, and Tasmanian devils.

Do Sugar Glider's Make Good Pets?

Sugar gliders can make excellent pets, but this greatly depends on the care they are given from their owner. Sugar gliders are extremely social animals, and as such, they require social interaction. If the owner cannot provide this social interaction on a regular basis, it is best not to own a sugar glider at all. This also means that sugar gliders should be kept in groups of two or more when owned as a pet. This allows your glider to have a friend no matter if you're swamped one day and cannot give them as much attention as they require. It should also be noted that no matter how much time you can devote to your glider, a glider companion can never be replaced by a human one.

You may not expect it of a pet, but sugar gliders are prone to depression when housed alone. So, if you're planning on getting one sugar glider, you really should be planning on getting at least two. With some sugar gliders, aggression and refusal to provide themselves with nourishment may also arise from being housed alone. This latter side effect can be extremely dangerous as it may cause your sugar glider to die of starvation and/or malnourishment.

Getting two or more sugar gliders doesn't mean that you have to get a male and a female, especially if you don't want breeding, and aren't willing to pay for getting them fixed. All female and/or all male groups are able to get along. That being said, it should be noted that all male groups should be taken in all at the same time, and should be from the same litter. This will eliminate the possibility of fighting, and make your life and their life much easier.

As mentioned earlier, the level of care provided by the owner makes a huge difference in how the sugar glider turns out. Essentially, whether your glider will be a great pet, or simply be a resident of the home. Even with a glider companion, sugar gliders should have ample human interaction. The level of interaction you provide will determine how friendly the glider turns out to be.

As with most pets, the best time to start interacting with a sugar glider is when the glider is a baby. During this time, the glider baby should be handled daily. This includes taking them out of the cage and holding them, cuddling with them, you can even create a pouch to carry them around in. When inside the cage, take the time to speak to your sugar glider and reach through the cage to give them pats on the head or strokes down the body. Every little bit of interaction helps to domesticate your glider and bond with them. The more handling you're able to do will help your glider feel completely comfortable around you.

All in all, sugar gliders make excellent pets, if you're ready for the level of commitment they require. Don't assume because sugar gliders are caged animals that they don't require a high level of attention. Instead, think of having a sugar glider (or preferably two) as having dogs. You need to take the time to bond with them, train them, give them exercise, and give them love. If you don't have the time to spend taking care of your pets, including cleaning the cage and all the items inside, then a sugar glider simply isn't a good fit for you.

Is A Sugar Glider The Right Pet For You?

Some Things For You To Consider...

1) Are you willing to commit to 12 – 14 years of pet ownership?
Sugar gliders have an average lifespan of 12 – 14 years. Of course, this is only the average, so you could have fewer or more depending on the glider.

2) Can you accommodate creatures that are naturally nocturnal?
Because sugar gliders are nocturnal, they are mainly active during the nighttime hours. This means they will be up and playing at night, possibly while you're trying to sleep. If this is going to bother you, then you should have a separate room for your sugar gliders so that they can play and you can sleep.

Sugar gliders need a lot of love, and one way to do that is carry and snuggle your sugar glider during the day. Often the glider will sleep in this pouch, but the time with them is completely necessary and very important.

3) Are you able to provide your sugar glider with playtime and bonding time?
Sugar gliders require a fairly significant amount of time to bond with their owners. You need to be able to dedicate this time in order to have a good experience with your pet. Additionally, sugar gliders need space to run around, so you need to have time to dedicate to taking them out of their cage and letting them run around.

4) Do you have the financial stability to provide for a sugar glider?

Sugar gliders are exotic pets, so they aren't cheap. Aside from having special dietary needs, veterinary care for gliders is extremely expensive. Getting a cage and all the necessary housing needs also isn't cheap, so be sure to take all expenses into consideration.

5) Can you accommodate a pair of sugar gliders?
Sugar gliders are extremely social creatures, and having one sugar glider is not recommended. Instead, it is highly recommended that you have two or more sugar gliders. Having only one, risks health difficulties and depression for your sugar glider.

6) Are sugar gliders legal to own in your state?
Sugar gliders are not legal in every state in the United States, so check and make sure that you're able to legally own one.

7) Is veterinary care available in your area?
Because sugar gliders are exotic pets, there isn't always veterinary care available for them. Look around and speak to a variety of different exotic pet veterinarians to ensure that you'll have veterinary care available to you.

8) Do you have other pets that may interfere with your ability to socialize with and/or otherwise care for a sugar glider?
We've already discussed how much time it takes to care for a sugar glider and this can interfere with caring for and playing with your other pets. Additionally, will other pets pose a risk to a sugar glider? Due to their small size, cats or dogs are not ideal housemates for them.

9) Is everyone in the house responsible enough to care for the sugar gliders?
Sugar gliders are not ideal pets for children. They are fragile and require special handling. They also require special bonding to learn to trust their owners, and children are often not patient enough to engage in this extensive bonding process. Additionally,

sugar glider cages need frequent changes (1 – 2 times per week), and children are often not responsible enough to ensure that this gets done. Failure to properly clean the cage can lead to illness.

10) Do you have a responsible and reliable pet sitter?
Having someone to care for your sugar gliders when out of town is essential. Because they require such a high level of care, sugar gliders are not ideal candidates for being left at home alone (even for a 24 hour period), and few kennels will take small exotic pets like sugar gliders. Additionally, you need to ensure that your sitter is aware of all the special needs of your pet and is able to meet all those needs.

What To Look For When Purchasing A Sugar Glider

Purchasing a sugar glider is much like purchasing any other pet, you want to make sure the animal looks healthy. No one wants to get a sick pet, or get a pet that passes shortly after purchase due to illness. So, to avoid this, it is important to evaluate potential sugar gliders before purchasing.

Signs that a sugar glider is healthy are:
- Bright unclouded eyes
- Eyes clear of any watering or goo
- Muscular body structure
- Clean, well cared for fur

If there are any problems or concerns when looking at sugar gliders ask the owner questions. If after all questions have been answered you are still unsure of the health of the glider, walk away and do not purchase. Sugar gliders are huge monetary investments as it is; the last thing you need is an unhealthy glider that requires veterinary care soon after getting it home.

Another thing to look at is temperament. While you will need to invest time in bonding with your sugar glider, they should have a good temperament to start with. Look for a glider that seems active and tolerates being handled well. Overly skittish or testy gliders may be able to be trained to be the happiest and most friendly pets you've ever had, or they can simply prove to be too much to handle. So, unless you have a great deal of experience handling and training sugar gliders, it is best to choose one that does well being handled and already seems to deal well with social situations.

Lastly, look at the seller. In order to sell baby sugar gliders, the U.S Department of Agriculture requires that the seller have an exotic pet license. Thus, if no license is present, pass up the seller and find a more reputable one. This may mean paying more than you were going to on the unlicensed breeder/seller, but it is for the best. Unlicensed sellers may cut corners in breeding and socializing. Additionally, buying from these sellers only encourages them to breed more. In order to only encourage safe breeding and selling, it is best to go about getting one from a completely legitimate seller.

Picking A Sugar Glider No-Nos

Choosing the right sugar glider is important and there are a lot of things to look for when picking the right glider for you. But just as there are imperatives to choosing a sugar glider, there are no-nos as well.

Bonding with a sugar glider takes a lot of work and dedication. There is a huge pay-off when you've bonded with it, but you really have to put in the time. That being said, don't expect that you'll be able to bond right off the bat when choosing a sugar glider. Don't expect that a new glider will want to cuddle with you. In fact, it is not advised that you try and put the glider right up to your face and cuddle and kiss it. The glider needs time to bond, and you're likely to get nipped at or growled at. This doesn't mean that the glider is aggressive or a poor fit, it just means that you've scared it. After all, you're quite a bit larger than it, and the poor little sugar glider may feel that you're trying to eat it.

One great way to get a feel for whether a particular glider is a good fit or not, is to hold it in your hand(s) for around 10 minutes. This is a rather long period of time, but it will allow the glider to calm down a bit, and then you can properly gauge whether it may be for you.

Another thing that tends to scare sugar gliders is making shushing noises and kissing noises at them. These sounds can sound very close to the sugar glider's natural "crabbing" noise, a defensive/aggressive noise, so it can be intimidating to them. Until you are more closely bonded with them, you should avoid making either of these noises, and stick to speaking to them in a very soft and comforting voice.

Along similar lines is the tendency of animal owners to look their pets directly in the eye. While this isn't often a problem with a well-bonded glider, trying this with a glider that is not familiar with and comfortable with you can greatly scare and intimidate it. Remember that these little pocket pets aren't exactly high on the totem pole in terms of the food chain. Staring at them in the eyes resembles the contact that is made with predators in the wild, and they may mistake your loving or interested stare for one of predation.

Taking Your Sugar Glider Home And Bonding

Getting any new pet requires a great deal of commitment, and getting a sugar glider is no different. Sugar gliders require a great deal of attention, and a very special bonding process. Because sugar gliders are marsupials it is important to remember that joeys (baby sugar gliders) are used to being snuggled comfortably in their mother's pouch. As such, having a pouch of your own ready and waiting for your new addition, hopefully additions, is extremely important.

Another must have before your joey gets home is a method to get your joey acclimated to your scent. Sugar gliders are extremely scent oriented, so getting them used to your scent is a great way to build trust and bond with your joey even when they aren't being handled. The best way to do this is to use several pieces of fabric, get your scent on them, and put one in your joey's sleeping pouch each day. You can purchase fabric for this purpose, or cut apart an old shirt or towel. Cut the fabric into small pieces, around 4 to 5 inches in size and tuck them into your shirt or somewhere close to your body. Many people choose to sleep like this, which gets your scent on the fabric. Once you wake up, place one piece in your joey's sleeping pouch, and the rest in a plastic bag for storage.

One reason why this is such a great idea is because a new sugar glider, joey or not, needs at least 24 hours in their new cage without being handled after you get them. Getting a new home is very stressful, so this period of time will help to distress your glider, as well as help them to acclimate to their new environment. Having your scent in their sleeping pouch will help to speed along the acclimation process.

Another way to help the process along is to spend some time in the first 24 hours to simply sit next to the cage and talk to your new glider. Again, this acclimates them to your scent, and it also helps them to get used to your voice. This will help your glider feel more comfortable as you go on with your life around it, and when you go to begin handling your sugar glider.

The next step in the bonding process is beginning to handle your sugar glider. This needs to be done slowly, and with a great deal of care. You don't want to stress or startle your new sugar glider. So, begin by keeping your joey in a sleeping pouch during the day, but keep the pouch close to you. Do this for a good period during the day when your glider is sleeping. This will help them further acclimate to your scent. After several days, begin to pet your glider from the outside of the pouch. You can begin by petting your glider by sticking your hand in the pouch, but many new gliders will nip, so it is often best to take very small steps in the handling process and begin petting on the outside of the pouch.

Next, choose a treat and reach inside the pouch and give it to your little critter. Offering treats is a great way to show that you mean well, and you mean to provide. Furthermore, the closeness allows for further scent acclimation. Treat options will be discussed a little later, but some treat ideas are dried or frozen fruit, applesauce, and fruit yogurt.

If your sugar glider is still jumpy and nips, regress to petting from outside the pouch and continue to place your scented fabric in the pouch. In some cases your sugar glider may nip at your finger not out of fear, but out of habit. This mainly happens when treating with applesauce, small dabs of honey, or yogurt that would be licked off the finger. Because sugar gliders suck sap from trees in the wild, they may assume that there are more treats to be had if they nip at your finger and suck from it. Be sure to pull your finger before the entire stock of treat is depleted to avoid this natural reflex.

The last step to the initial acclimation process is petting your sugar glider from inside the pouch. When your sugar glider seems comfortable enough with your petting him from outside the pouch, and with reaching in to give him treats, try reaching in and petting him. If your sugar glider nips, regress to step one, and work up to this stage again. Some sugar gliders are extremely easy going and are thus easier to train. Other gliders require a great deal more care and may take longer to fully acclimate to their new home and you. Give them time and be as understanding and gentle as possible. Be sure to give them ample opportunity to smell you and hear your voice so they know you as a friend, instead of as a threat. A lot of sugar glider owners like to carry around their pouched gliders as they go about their day in the home. This is a great way for them to get used to you. Just remember that safety comes first. Don't take them anywhere that you think they may get hurt or get loose, and be sure to handle them carefully.

When you're able to pet them comfortably, and they seem at ease with you petting them, you're ready to begin interacting with them when they are outside of their sleeping pouch. The best way to start this process is by giving them tent time.

Tent time is a method which utilizes a tent to offer a controlled atmosphere in which you and your sugar glider can interact outside of the cage and pouch. To do this, you'll need a tent. Purchase a medium sized pup tent.

Stores like Walmart and Target have them for very cheap, you don't need anything fancy. Set the tent up in your room, or any other room with enough space for it. Once the tent is up, and you have an hour or two to dedicate to tent time with your pet, bring the glider into the tent in its pouch. You can also bring in a lantern or flashlight for extra light.

If there is a netted window, you can open that as well for light and airflow. Once in, settle in and pull your glider from their pouch and set them in the tent. You may set them in your lap or next to you. From here on out, keep yourself busy. Don't reach out to your sugar glider. Instead, allow him/her to come to you. Over time, your glider with get used to you and will come to check you out. Enough time and you'll notice he/she wants to hang around with you and cuddle with you.

Some sugar gliders warm up to their owners more easily than others. This means that some gliders may want cuddling and attention within the first day. Others may need a week or more of tent time before they feel comfortable. Give them the time they need. If they are skittish and timid around you, don't push them. Eventually they will come to you and feel comfortable enough around you to want to spend time with you. Continue tent time even if things are going well.

This time is extremely important to bonding, and will help your glider come to you when out of their cage and out of the tent. The goal is to be able to allow the glider to hang out with you in your room without the use of a tent to contain them. If your sugar glider isn't comfortable with you, this will be highly impractical as it will be impossible to get him/her back in their cage, let alone spend any time with them while out of their cage.

Bonding Sugar Gliders With Other Pets

So, you want a sugar glider, or possibly already have one, and you also have other pets. How do you go about bonding your sugar glider to your other pets? Well, the good news is that sugar gliders are extremely friendly and extremely sociable. Chances are, your sugar glider will take to your other pets right away. What is more likely to be necessary is that your other pets will need to be bonded with, and acclimated to, your sugar glider.

First, a little on sugar gliders. As previously mentioned, sugar gliders are extremely social animals. In their natural habitat, they live in colonies that often have up to fifteen members. While your glider may initially be a bit apprehensive of you and the other pets in your home, over time, and with bonding (through the cage, tent time, and out of the cage) sugar gliders come to see you and the other pets in the home as part of their own little colony. In fact, failure to bond with, and spend enough time with your sugar glider, will result in your glider feeling isolated, lonely, and depressed. Sugar gliders that experience this often self-harm, become lethargic, and rarely venture from their pouches. In severe cases, your glider may simply fail to care for its basic needs and die. So, your task is to make this come as easy as possible. Your task is to make your glider feel that you, and the other pets in the home are friends and not threats.

We've already discussed bonding with your sugar glider, and this is extremely important. This should occur before you fully introduce any other pets to your sugar glider. Essentially, with proper bonding, your sugar glider will come to see you as a comforting source of friendship, as well as a source of security. So, give them a couple weeks for this to occur. As you work to bond with your sugar glider in and out of the cage, allow any other pets in the home access to the glider cage. This does not mean you should allow them in the cage, just that they should be able to walk up to the cage and see inside. Just as with you, this allows your sugar glider to become acclimated to the scent of your other pets. Similarly, this allows your other pets to become acclimated to the sugar glider.

Be sure you have a proper and safe cage. With the right cage, your other pets will not have enough physical space to reach through and hurt your new sugar glider, but will be able to sniff the cage and glider. In some cases, your existing pets may be standoffish or even aggressive. Typically this passes fairly quickly. If the glider feels threatened, it will engage in a behavior called crabbing. This is a behavior in which the sugar glider stands on its hind legs, puts its little arms in the air, and squeals loudly. This sound and behavior expresses that the sugar glider is uncomfortable and/or feels threatened.

As your glider begins to have more time around your other pets (as well as you), you'll see and hear this less and less. If you continue to experience crabbing toward either you or your pets, you need to spend some serious time bonding. Go back to step one of bonding and work up, because this is a clear indicator that your sugar glider is not at all comfortable with you or the other pets of the house.

As time passes sugar gliders and other pets in the home tend to acclimate, and even bond, very well. It should be noted that some pets will simply never fully bond with your glider. However, experts and seasoned sugar glider owners agree that nearly all (we're talking 95% or so) of other pets will bond well with your sugar glider. Some pets (such as dogs and cats) bond so well that they become very close. Not only is this great for you as the owner of both, but it's great for the glider as they have a lifelong friend to hang with.

Another pet can be a great source for companionship and comfort for a sugar glider. This is one reason why it is recommended that you purchase sugar gliders in pairs. It is not uncommon for bonded pets to hang out together, even when the sugar glider is in its cage.

When To Introduce Other House Pets

Choosing when to introduce your other pets face to face to your sugar glider is a very serious and important decision. Through the cage introductions are important, but not nearly as critical and serious as the face to face introduction. When out of the cage, both pets are more likely to feel a little more apprehensive and threatened. This is why it is extremely important to give them ample time to get used to each other with the cage as a barrier between them.

The good news is that sugar gliders and other pets tend to react to one another face to face in a way that is very similar to the way in which they react to one another through the cage. Although this is often the case, it is still important to carefully choose a time, and carefully monitor the meeting. So, be sure to watch the interactions between your other pet and your sugar glider when they meet through the cage. I say meet here, but I mean each time they encounter one another, not simply the first time. If after ten times of meeting your sugar glider is still crabbing, or even a little apprehensive, give the two pets more time together through the cage before moving on to face to face interaction.

If, after ten days, the interaction between the two animals seems amiable, both seem comfortable, and there is no aggressive or apprehensive behavior, you can begin to consider a face to face meeting.

Once you decide that the two should interact outside of the cage, it is time to choose a method for their meeting. You want to carefully monitor and control the meeting, so holding the sugar glider, or your other pet, loosely throughout the meeting is a good idea. In this way, you're there to stop or prevent any problems before they occur. As more time goes on, the two pets are likely to form an inseparable bond. Glider owners all over the world have hundreds of cute stories of their sugar gliders playing with and cuddling with the other pets of the house. With patience, your two pets will also be the best of friends!

Sugar Glider Behaviors, Sounds And Their Meaning

We've discussed some typical sugar glider behaviors already, but this section will serve to further discuss, review, and introduce new behaviors for you to look out for. Understanding your sugar glider's behaviors will help you to better understand, communicate with, and care for your sugar glider.

Crabbing

This is both a behavior and sound that the sugar glider makes to express fear and aggression. It is seen and heard when your glider is uncertain, and most of all feels threatened. It is not at all uncommon to experience this when you first get your sugar glider since they are not familiar with, or bonded with, you. Similarly, sugar gliders may do this to other pets in the home who they are not bonded with or acclimated to.

Crabbing sounds like a loud screeching type noise. Some sugar glider owners describe it as an almost dying machine-like nose. This loud noise is most often accompanied by the glider standing on its two hind legs and putting its front arms into the air. This is generally done within close proximity to the source of the threat (i.e. you or another pet) in order to intimidate them, shock them, or throw them off so the sugar glider has time to get away.

Biting

This is most commonly seen in baby gliders, or when a glider feels threatened. This can also follow crabbing if the threat that caused the crabbing continues.

Biting, or trying to bite, a person or other pet is a defense mechanism.

Nipping

Nipping is a completely different behavior than biting. Sugar gliders typically nip in order to taste something. It is very common for a glider to nip because they'd like to interact with something in their environment by tasting it. Additionally, nipping may indicate hunger, or the desire for a treat. As you own your glider you may be able to recognize which of these desires the glider is trying to communicate by nipping. The important thing to note is that this is a completely friendly behavior. They are not trying to hurt you, they're just curious, or wanting you to treat them!

Head Rubbing

Just when you thought your glider couldn't get any cuter, you experience the head rub. This is a very friendly behavior that occurs when your glider is well bonded to you. This behavior includes your glider taking your hand, finger, or something else nearby with its little hands, curling its head toward its belly, and then rubbing its head against you. This may be followed up by it rubbing its body against you.

Head and body rubbing is a very friendly behavior, and is thought to be a welcome, a thank you, and/or a hello. Sugar gliders do this to one another lovingly, so you should feel blessed to have them do it to you as well.

Chirping

Chirping is exactly what it sounds like. This is a sound that sugar gliders make to express that they are happy ad comfortable. You may hear chirping when your sugar glider is being pet, is being cuddled, or is eating a favorite treat.

Purring

This is generally a very easy sound for humans to understand because it is easily likened to the feline purr. Like the purring of a cat, sugar gliders purr to express happiness.

Sneeze-like Noise

This sound is strange, but best described as sounding like a sneeze. It is generally heard when a sugar is telling you, or another glider (most commonly) that something is theirs. In other words, it is a sort of territorial thing.

Barking

Barking isn't just reserved for dogs, sugar gliders also bark. The bark of a sugar glider is not a loud noise, but is often likened to the sound of a dog's bark off in the distance. Barking is a communication of anger with other gliders, or a means of expressing fear. Other gliders in the room will react to a bark by taking cover or freezing in place. If you are well bonded with your sugar glider, you may become a source of protection for them, so don't be surprised if barking is accompanied by your sugar gliders running to you for protection.

Grooming

When your glider s very well bonded to you, you'll probably notice that they lick you and try to pull things off your clothes and skin. This may be a band-aid or a scab, just anything that they don't recognize and instead see as a foreign body. This is a loving behavior and simply means that you're part of the clan and very important to them.

Squawk

If you have a baby sugar glider, you're most likely to hear this noise coming from them. This is a sound made when the baby is distressed and calling out for help. This typically means they are calling out for mom and/or dad. If mom and dad are not present, you will need to step in and comfort them if possible.

Giggling or Gurgling

The giggling or gurgling noise you hear from your glider is another means of expressing happiness, comfort, and being content. This is often heard when a glider is being pet, is munching on a favorite treat, or is being held or cuddled.

Feeding Your Sugar Glider

Dietary Needs

Diet is a very important part of a sugar glider's health, so meeting their special dietary needs is essential in having a healthy, happy, sugar glider. Failure to properly feed your sugar glider can result in disease, lack of energy, and depression.

While bagged foods are available for purchase through pet stores that deal in exotic pet supplies, it is not recommended that pre-bagged foods are offered as the only source of nutrition for your sugar glider. Instead, it is recommended that a special blend of food be mixed at home and offered to your sugar glider. There are several recipes for the blending of the right sugar glider diet that can be used, and these will be discussed. Also to be discussed in this section are the feeding routines and proportions necessary for a healthy, happy sugar glider.

Before we delve into what and how to feed your sugar glider, it is important to understand what sorts of dietary needs a sugar glider has. Although sugar gliders are small mammals, only about the size of a hamster, they are not herbivores, as many people assume. Sugar gliders are actually omnivores, feeding on vegetables, fruit, and insects. In fact, insects make up a rather large portion of the sugar glider diet, often earning the title of insectivore instead of omnivore.

In addition to a large amount of insects, wild sugar gliders eat acacia gum, eucalyptus sap, and other plant nectars, especially during the winter months when insects are in lower abundance. Also a favorite are manna and honeydew. Manna is a sugar that is found on the trunks and/or branches of trees where sap flowed from the tree; and honeydew is a sugar that is produced, and left behind, by insects that feed on the sap of the trees.

To make up for this natural diet, insects should also be a part of your pet glider's diet. This often takes the form of mealworms for many sugar glider owners. Additionally, honey, nectars, and fresh fruits are used to sub for the sugary saps that sugar gliders enjoy in the wild.

The key to a successful dietary regimen is to ensure that you use variety to meet your sugar glider's needs. No one vegetable or fruit has all the vitamins needed, so it is important that you mix up what fruits and vegetables are offered in order to deliver all the necessary vitamins and minerals. This helps to greatly prevent disease, and ensures that your sugar glider has all the energy it needs to function. In addition to variety, it is important to take into account what your pet likes. Just like people, sugar gliders have preferences on foods. If you notice that your pet isn't eating a particular type of food, cut it from your glider's diet and find a different item that provides the same nutritional value.

Sugar Gliders

A Balanced Diet

A balanced diet is important for your sugar glider. A balanced sugar glider diet consists of a source of protein, a source of fresh fruit and vegetable, a vitamin supplement, and a grazing or snacking food.

Proteins

Protein source ideas: mealworms, crickets, grasshoppers, eggs, yogurt. Proteins can be rotated on a daily basis so that your sugar glider has a revolving menu. Portions for each protein are as follows (2):

Mealworms – 10 to 12 small worms per glider. If your local pet store only has the larger varieties serve 7 to 10 medium sized mealworms, or 3 to 5 large mealworms. Again, this is per sugar glider. So, for two sugar gliders, you'll need around 20 to 24 small mealworms.

Crickets – Offer around 5 crickets per sugar glider. A comparable number of grasshoppers can be used, so long as the size is approximately the same.

Mealworms and crickets purchased at typical pet stores are often undernourished. This means that if you're feeding them to your sugar gliders, your gliders are missing out on a great deal of nourishment. The solution? Gut-loading the insects before giving them to your pets. Although the name sounds odd, gut-loading is actually the simple act of feeding the insects for 24-48 hours before giving them to your sugar gliders. This means that you're feeding your gliders the best protein option out there, instead of offering protein that is void of much of the nourishment that gliders would get in the wild. Gut-loading feed can be found at local pet stores, as well as online.

Eggs – Can be boiled or scrambled. If boiled cut the egg up before serving it. Whether cut up or scrambled, serve around one tablespoon of egg per sugar glider. Don't bother leveling off the tablespoon as an over-full tablespoon is about the right amount.

Yogurt – Blueberry and peach are the preferred flavors for yogurt serving. Yogurt should be served in one full tablespoon for a pair of sugar gliders.

It should be noted that baby sugar gliders or joeys do have slightly different dietary restrictions. This is because they are too immature to handle some of the foods that a more mature sugar glider can handle. The main restriction here is that insects like mealworms, crickets, and grasshoppers are a bit too advanced for a joey. As the joey grows, you can start offering small mealworms and monitoring to see that it can handle and eat the worm with no trouble. Until that time, substitute mealworms and other insects with human baby food, such as baby food chicken.

Another caution concerning the use of mealworms and crickets is a mold known as "aflatoxin." Aflatoxin can be found in the bedding that is used when housing crickets and mealworms. Unfortunately, this mold can be extremely toxic to sugar gliders. The problem is that when crickets or mealworms ingest, or carry on their bodies, the mold found in their cage, it can be passed to the sugar glider when they eat the insect.

Aflatoxin greatly affects the liver of the sugar glider, making them unable to cleanse the body of the mold poisoning, causing serious illness, and often death. It is difficult to determine whether this mold is found in the bedding used to raise and house crickets and mealworms, so ask your source directly. Most typically, this mold is found in corn bedding, so avoid purchasing any insects for your sugar gliders from places that use corn-based bedding.

Fresh Fruits And Vegetables

The key word here is fresh, and this means that fruit and vegetable offerings may not only vary by nutritional value, but by season. Get what you can, and don't sweat it too much if something is too expensive or simply unavailable. Some fruit and vegetable sources are apples, blueberries, kiwi, mango, pear, sweet potato, carrots, and honeydew. Oranges can also be a great option in moderation. Suggested dose of oranges is once a week at the most. Joeys are not allowed to have oranges at all, so don't offer it to them until they are more mature.

Portions for fruit and vegetables are about one slice to each pair of gliders. These should be on the small side. Don't slice too thick or too large. Remember that your sugar glider is very small, and they don't need to over indulge in fruit and vegetables. Too much fruit or vegetables can lead to obesity and other health difficulties.

Vitamins

Even with your offerings of fresh fruits and vegetables, your sugar glider will require that you provide them with a vitamin and mineral supplement. These supplements should be given daily to provide the best possible nutrition. There are a variety of vitamins that work for this purpose, include dog, cat, and reptile vitamins.

Vionate is a vitamin and mineral supplement that comes recommended (2) by top sugar glider care sites and veterinarians. It is made specifically for small mammals, and is excellent for sugar gliders when combined with an added source of calcium. Rep-Cal calcium (2) is one calcium supplement of choice, but similar products will work as well.

Extra calcium is extremely important for sugar gliders due to their nocturnal nature, which can cause serious bone issues. In fact, calcium deficiencies are one of the major health issues experienced by pet sugar gliders. As such it is extremely important to take this need into account when planning your sugar glider's diet.

Another important point to note when choosing a calcium supplement is that sugar gliders need a phosphorus free version.

Furthermore, vitamin D is often present in calcium in order to help the body process it, but since you'll be giving your glider a multi-vitamin supplement as well, you won't need extra vitamin D, so be sure that you're getting calcium only. Like humans, it is possible for sugar gliders to overdose on vitamins, so it is important that you're careful in choosing your vitamin supplements, and in administering them.

The easiest way to administer these vitamin supplements is to sprinkle a very small amount, about a pinch (2) of each onto the fruit and vegetable choices for the day. This will provide your sugar glider with ample vitamins and minerals, without over-feeding them.

Grazing/Snacking Food

Because sugar gliders eat a great deal of fresh foods, pulling their foods after mealtime is essential to avoid allowing your glider to ingest old or rotting food. However, just because mealtime is over doesn't mean that your glider isn't going to be a bit hungry throughout the day. For this, having some spoil-safe snack foods is essential.

Snacks are a little less strict than other meal requirements, and there are a great deal of options. The most highly recommended by experienced sugar glider owners and veterinarians are those that are based on animal proteins. This comes from the fact that sugar gliders consume so many insects in the wild, and as such, protein from animal (or insect) sources is extremely important. Some options for snacks are as follows:

- **ZooKeeper's Secret**: A wet food snacking or grazing option. This is pre-mixed and can be kept in your sugar glider's cage between feedings for grazing or snacking purposes.

- Wholesome Balance Chicken and Brown Rice Blend: A dry food that utilizes animal protein as a primary ingredient. This allows for the food to be able to sit longer without it needing to be replaced frequently as wet foods like the ZooKeeper's Secret do.

- **Indigenous Australian Foliage**: Because sugar gliders would consume these in the wild, it is important to have them available for consumption throughout the day. Indigenous plants foliage that sugar gliders would eat are acacia, callistemon, eucalyptus, and banksia. Check with your local nurseries for these plants. If they are not available locally, there are many online options to obtain them for your sugar glider.

Treating Your Sugar Glider

Treating your sugar glider is just as important as feeding. It not only makes for a very happy sugar glider, it is also a great way to bond with them. However, there is no point in treating a sugar glider if it's going to make them sick, so learning the right treats, and the right portions is important. If there is any doubt as to your treating regimen, consult a veterinarian.

Some great options for treating include:
- Eucalyptus branches
- Yogurt drops
- Dried papaya, bananas, and mangoes
- Honey sticks
- Diced coconut
- Goji Berries (dried or fresh)
- Insects (mealworms and crickets)
- Apple bites (fresh applies diced)
- Carob drops (sweet like chocolate, but contains none so it is completely safe)
- Dried carrots
- Glider biscuits (dry or soaked in apple juice)
- Gumivore (an acacia gum based treat)

Sugar Glider Enrichment

In addition to providing a healthy diet and some treats to break up the monotony of the daily food offerings, sugar gliders need some additional enrichment. These items not only help to entertain the glider, but work similar to treats to help shake things up.

Tree Branches

Tree branches provide gliders with something to chew on. This helps to break up the boredom of hanging out in a cage all day long. Additionally, it allows for the gliders to have items in the cage to climb all over. Tree branches can be purchased at any local pet store in the small pet section. Apple wood is the best to get as it tastes great, and is sugar glider safe. Eucalyptus branches are also a sugar glider favorite. In some cases, branches in these varieties are available with a metal attachment to make using it as a climbing device easier. These are great as they provide a safe, stationary perch and chewing option.

Gliderade

This is a mixture that can be purchased at stores dealing in sugar glider materials, or online through reputable sugar glider pet shops. Gliderade provides additional carbohydrates to sugar gliders, which works to support their extremely fast metabolic rate. Additionally, the taste is reminiscent of the nectars they'd be having in the wild, so it greatly enhances their environment.

Acacia Gum

Acacia gum is something wild sugar gliders love, and most caged ones also greatly enjoy it. This can be used as a treat, or as a regular enhancement to their diet. Leave small amounts of acacia gum in a ceramic dish (heavy enough so that it cannot be tipped over). Your gliders will love finding this here and there throughout the week.

Your Glider's Main Entrée Recipes

High Protein Recipe (1)

What you'll need:
- 2 cups of warm water
- 1 ½ cups of honey
- 3 eggs (scrambled)
- 1 Tbsp. bee pollen (Australian or American)
- ¼ cup of high protein wombaroo powder (HWP)

Putting it together:
Stir together the water and honey until the honey is completely dissolved into the water. Once the honey is dissolved, add in the HPW powder. Set this mixture aside and scramble the 3 eggs. This can be done on the stovetop or in the microwave, as desired. Once the eggs are done put them into a blender with the bee pollen and a small portion of the water/honey/HPW mixture (around 1 cup), and mix well. Slowly add the rest of the water/honey/HPW mixture, and again mix well. Once everything is combined, put it into a plastic airtight tub and place in the freezer. This will freeze up to resemble ice cream.

1.5 teaspoons of the HPW mixture should be given to each sugar glider daily. This mixture is meant to be served with fresh fruits and vegetables and daily treats as follows:
- 1 Tbsp. of mixed fruit
- 1 Tbsp. of mixed vegetables
- Mealworm treats
- Gliderade twice a week (1)

See references and resources section for source of recipe and ingredients.

Suncoast Diet (2)

This diet was developed, and is used by the Suncoast Sugar Glider breeders, a very reputable group. The diet was specifically developed by a veterinarian, and is highly recommended throughout the sugar glider owning world. The one downside is all the fresh food that is used, as this may be more costly than mixing frozen or dried foods into the daily meal routine.

Gliders on this diet are meant to follow a three part menu, consisting of a protein source, a fruit and/or vegetable source, and a staple food. It is also based on a 4 day rotation of offerings in order to keep the gliders from getting bored with their diet too easily.

Protein offerings per glider:
- *Mealworms*:
10-12 small worms, 7-10 medium worms, or 3-5 larger worms
Each worm is gut loaded for maximum nutrition

- *Yogurt* (typically blueberry or peach flavored):
1 ½ teaspoons (heaping teaspoons)

- *Crickets*:
3-5 crickets
Gut loaded for maximum nutrition

- *Boiled eggs*
Peel off the shell as gliders should not have this
Crumble egg and mix it with corn flake cereal and honey.
Serve 1 ½ teaspoon of this mixture.

Fruit and Vegetable Offerings:
The Suncoast diet rotates a number of different fruits and vegetables, including, but not limited to: apples, watermelon, pears, honeydew, carrots, blueberries, and cantaloupe. These fruit offerings are limited to portions of about the size of 1/8 of an

apple. See the resources section later in the book for longer list of sugar glider safe fruit offerings.

Vitamin and Mineral Supplement Offerings:
The Suncoast diet specifically uses Vionate and Rep-Cal Calcium (phosphorus free, D3 free) . These are sprinkled on the fruits and vegetables that are given each day.

It should be noted with this diet that it is especially important to pull old food from the cage every morning, or as it is noticed that fruit and vegetables are getting dry, shriveled, and/or brown. Fresh food is important for your sugar gliders and bad or rotten foods can cause major problems for your glider. So, feeding at night and pulling old food in the morning is highly preferred for this diet.

Judie's Modified BML Recipe (3)

Judie's Modified BML Recipe is a BML modification that was created by Judie Hausmann. The modifications were made to the diet to make it healthier for sugar gliders, as well as easier to feed as a sugar glider pet owner, as opposed to a zoo keeper where more options are available.

Preparation Instructions:
Blend together ½ cup of honey, one boiled egg (without the shell), and ¼ cup of mixed fruit juice. This mixed fruit juice can be any fresh blend of fruits you choose.

After blending, add one four ounce Gerber juice to the blender, as well as ½ teaspoon of Rep-Cal Herpivite vitamin supplement. Blend this mixture again until all ingredients are mixed in.

Next, add to the blender two teaspoons of Rep-Cal calcium supplement (phosphorus free), two small (2 ½ ounce) jars of chicken baby food, ½ cup of baby cereal (dry), and ¼ cup of wheat germ. Blend thoroughly, and then put into ice cube trays and freeze. This is easiest if portioned into the ice cube tray in one tablespoon portions if one glider is owned. For two gliders, the standard ice cube tray is around two tablespoons per cube. Be sure to test your tray before serving to be sure you've got the right portions. Once this is established, you won't need to keep doing this over and over again.

Feeding:
Each sugar glider will get one tablespoon of the Judie's mix, in addition to: one tablespoon of fruit, and one tablespoon of vegetables. Frozen fruits and vegetables can be used for this portion, which helps in storage and in saving money. However, fresh fruits and vegetables can also be used as desired.

Homemade Glider Nectar
Water
Frozen Fruit (any variety that is safe can be used. Blueberries are highly recommended for their nutritional value)
Yogurt (plain and without artificial sweeteners)

Preparation:
Choices on portions are up to you, but keep in mind small batches are best. Blend frozen fruit with water and yogurt. Feed immediately. This may be saved in the fridge for a day or so, but fresh is best for your glider.

Watering Your Sugar Glider

Although watering your sugar glider seems like one of the easiest parts of owning them, dehydration is one of the biggest, and most common problems among these little pocket pets. As such, it is important to not only provide adequate liquids for hydration, but also be sure they know where to find these liquids.

The largest threat for dehydration in a sugar glider occurs when they are babies. At this stage, your glider will not drink unless you show them where water is, and prompt them to drink. This can be done both while they are in their cage, and while you're carrying them in their pouch. While in the cage, you need to guide your glider to the location of the water and watch them drink. Choose a location near where they sleep often so they can easily find it. It is also highly recommended that water (as well as food) be placed in several locations around the cage for the easiest access possible.

The same principle applies to gliders that are being carried around for long periods of time. It is highly recommended that you carry your glider around with you in a pouch for much of the day (or at least as much as is possible). This is especially the case with baby gliders that need more boding time. However, this can also lead to dehydration if you don't take the time to pull them from the pouch and offer water. When doing this, place a dish of water in front of them and slightly press their nose into it so that they know it is water. Be sure to watch them drink.

This is extremely important because if you're not presenting the water correctly, your glider may be confused or refuse it, and this can lead to dehydration and even death. Sugar gliders have an extremely small body size, so it is extremely important for them to remain hydrated at all times.

Water bottles can be used as well, and these are sometimes preferred for gliders because they eliminate the risk of drowning.

It may sound dumb, but a glider can drown in a water bowl, just as human babies may drown in a tiny tub or sink very easily. The only trick to a water bottle is making sure that your sugar glider knows how to use it.

As with the presenting a water bowl, you need to present the water bottle to your sugar glider as well. This will be done in the same way as you would with a bowl. You need to take your glider to the water bottle, then press its little nose against the tip. This will cause a little water to come out. You may need to do this more than once, but the best way to ensure that your glider remembers this experience, and where to find the water is to give the water a sweet taste.

Adding this desired sweet taste is as easy as adding Gatorade or Pedialyte to the water. Start off by creating a water bottle mixture of half Gatorade/Pedialyte, and half water. These solutions work better than simply adding sugar because they not only add a sweet taste to the water, but also contain added electrolytes that work to hydrate the body. In fact, veterinarians often recommend Pedialyte to any pet that is experiencing hydration issues (i.e. vomiting or diarrhea); and doctors often recommend Pedialyte to babies for the same reasons.

As your sugar glider comes back to the water bottle repeatedly to drink, keep an eye on the level of the water. This will give you a good idea of how much they are drinking a day. When it is empty, refill, but this time use less Gatorade or Pedialyte. Keep adding less and less until your glider is just drinking plain water. You can offer the Gatorade/Pedialyte mix any time you think your pet isn't getting enough liquids to help hydrate, but otherwise, plain water is more than sufficient.

Water From Other Sources

Providing clean water isn't the only way to keep your sugar glider hydrated, in fact, gliders can get additional water from their diet. Sugar gliders need fruit for a variety of reasons, one being that they provide a decent amount of water. While fruit cannot be substituted for water bottle, it does make a great supplement. This is especially true when you have your sugar glider out in its pouch all day. If you're not able to set out a water dish for a bit, keep sliced apples on hand. A nice juicy apple is a great way to help your glider stay hydrated. Not to mention, they love the sweet taste! It makes for a great way to both hydrate and bond.

Sugar Glider Illnesses

One part of creating a strong bond with your sugar glider is helping it to stay healthy. Just as with humans, the best way to stay healthy is to be educated on potential problems, and the signs and symptoms associated with them.

Trichomoniasis

Trichomoniasis is a bacterial infection that can be caused by ingesting food and/or water that is contaminated by the trichomonas bacteria. Signs and symptoms of a glider with trichomoniasis include:
- Loss of appetite
- Weight loss
- Vomiting
- Diarrhea and/or other changes in the glider feces. These changes may include a change in color from the standard brown to a more golden color, the presences of mucus, and the presence of undigested food particles.

Trichomoniasis is treated by quarantining the infected pet, thoroughly cleansing the items that had contact with the infected pet (including the cage, watering bowl or bottle, toys, sleeping materials, etc). If other pets had contact, it is important to have them examined as well as they may have been infected but may not yet be showing symptoms. If they are not also infected, keep them in a separate cage from the infected pet.

It is also important to seek veterinary care for the infected pet as soon as possible. Because of their small body size, infection is extremely serious in a sugar glider. Once diagnosed with trichomoniasis, the pet will be prescribed antibiotics to fight and kill the bacteria. You must administer these medications exactly as directed in order to make them most effective.

It should also be noted here that trichomoniasis can also be passed on to humans, so care should be taken in handling the infected pet. Wash hands and clothing that have come in contact with both the sugar glider and its fecal matter.

Giardiasis

Giardiasis is an intestinal infection caused by a parasite. This can affect both pets and humans, so caution and care should be taken with this infection, as with trichomoniasis. Giardiasis is a tough infection to detect because it can lay dormant in the body around six months with no symptoms present. In cases like this, the glider may suffer extreme infection and/or death within a very short period, sometimes as short as a couple of hours. This is one reason why regular veterinary checkups are highly recommended.

As discussed, Giardiasis is caused by a parasite that is transmitted through the feces of an infected human or animal. The infection is contracted with the animal ingests food or other items that have had contact with the infected feces, and had not been cooked to kill the bacteria. This means that the uncooked fruits and vegetables that you feed to your sugar glider may be infected, and properly cleansing all foods given to your glider will help to prevent Giardiasis infection.

The signs and symptoms of a Giardiasis infection include:
- Vomiting
- Diarrhea
- Jaundice (yellowing of the skin and eyes indicating enlargement of the liver)
- Changes in fecal color from its normal shade to green
- Changes is typical glider behavior
- Dehydration

As with other medical issues, seeking medical care as soon as any signs and symptoms are present is extremely important. Even if only one symptom is present it is important to act on it right away and seek veterinary care. The sooner care is sought and received, the higher the chances that the glider will survive the infection

Once diagnosed, the infected glider needs to be quarantined right away, and all other gliders in the home need to be tested as well. Additionally, all items that have come in contact with the infected sugar glider and/or his/her feces need to be cleaned thoroughly, including the cage, toys, food and water dishes and bottles, and all bedding. Lastly, you will likely be responsible for treating the parasite infection with anti parasitic medication.

Constipation

Constipation is a condition in which it is difficult to have bowel movements, and bowel movements are small, hard, and/or dry. Constipation may also make it painful for your pet to have a bowel movement. Constipation can be caused by a number of factors, including:
- Dehydration
- Lack of proper fiber in the glider's daily diet
- Stress
- Lack of ample exercise
- Lack of ample vitamins and minerals in the diet (i.e. poor diet)
- Pain medications
- Dysfunction in the gastrointestinal tract

Signs and symptoms of constipation include:
- Pain with bowel movements (which may be experienced as crying, squealing, or straining).
- A decrease in the amount of feces being passed on a daily basis
- A lack of bowel movements

Constipation in a sugar glider is treated in much the same way that it is treated in humans, especially human babies. Add fibrous foods to their diet, such as prunes, and apples. Prune juice or orange juice can also be added to the water to assist in alleviating constipation. In addition to taking these steps, it is also important to seek medical care. While you may assume that you have the problem under control, and that it is only minor, constipation can signal a more serious problem, or become more serious itself. So, to be safe, seek medical assistance and medical advice to care for your glider as best as possible.

Calcium Deficiency and Hind Leg Paralysis

Calcium deficiency is exactly what it sounds like, the lack of ample calcium in the system. This lack of calcium can lead to a serious and potentially deadly infection called hind leg paralysis. Calcium deficiency is caused by a diet that has a poor calcium to phosphorous ratio, which is surprisingly common since many of the fruits and vegetables fed to gliders have low calcium levels. In these cases, a calcium supplement should be given to assist in maintaining appropriate calcium levels, avoiding deficiency, and avoiding hind leg paralysis

Calcium deficiency doesn't have any signs and symptoms on its own, and hind leg paralysis may occur before you realize your glider is calcium deficient. This is where regular veterinary checkups come in handy. Additionally, calcium-rich foods, and/or calcium supplements need to be given on a regular basis

Hind leg paralysis is a more complicated condition than just being a result of calcium deficiency, and can be the symptom of an even more serious condition. Causes of hind leg paralysis are the lack of proper calcium intake.

Signs and symptoms of hind leg paralysis include:
- Body tremors
- Limping
- Lethargy
- Paralysis
- Fractured bones
- Body weakness
- Inability to grip or having trouble griping
- Favoring one of the hind legs more than the other, and/or complete loss of both hind legs

The treatment for hind leg paralysis is to create a nutritional plan that will add the appropriate amount of calcium into the diet. However, it isn't as easy as doing this at home. A veterinarian is necessary to test for why calcium may be low (nutritional only, calcium being leached from the bones), finding the right calcium supplements and doses, and possible hospitalization until treatment is shown to be effective

The good news is that hind leg paralysis is reversible, and often sugar gliders that are treated amply and quickly, even the paralysis of the hind legs can be reversed and the glider can return to normal

Aflatoxicosis

Aflatoxicosis is a liver infection caused by ingesting contaminated corn, peanuts, or insects that are contaminated through their feed by aflatoxins. Sugar gliders are most at risk for aflatoxicosis when they are fed insects such as crickets and mealworms that are fed a corn-based diet.

Signs and symptoms of aflatoxicosis include:
- Anemia
- Lethargy
- Loss of appetite
- Changes in bowel movements (including diarrhea, changes in frequency, and changes in color)
-Jaundice of the eyes and skin

Treatment for aflatoxicosis include immediate medical care with the appearance of symptoms, and changing the nutrition that is being provided (finding new insects that are not contaminated, removing corn and peanuts). While aflatoxicosis is reversible when caught in time, it can also be deadly if not caught in time. Any changes at all in the behaviors or norms of your pet should be noted, and your pet needs to be taken to the vet.

Depression

At several points in this book we've discussed depression. This frequency of discussion is to emphasize that depression is a very real, and very serious problem for the social sugar glider. Depression not only presents on its own, but can also lead to other serious issues like illness and self-mutilation, not to mention death

Depression is a sugar glider can be caused by a number of factors, including:

- Neglect (owner not paying enough attention to glider, not taking the glider out enough)
- Lack of company during the day (having only one sugar glider)
- Death of companion gliders
- Episodes of prolonged illness

Signs and symptoms of depression include:
- Changes in sleep patterns (often resulting in excessive sleep)
- Changes in communication patterns (less vocal, fewer barks)
- Lack of interest in activities they used to find fun (no interest in playing or in toys)
- Decreased overall level of activity
- Pacing around the cage, or back flipping frequently

Treatment for depression can be both simple and complex. Because depression often results when one glider dies, or when you're raising only one glider, getting another glider can be the best solution. However, when getting a second sugar glider, it is important to properly introduce and socialize them before leaving them alone together.

Because sugar gliders are so social, this isn't typically too difficult, but it does need to be done. Another option is to step up the frequency in which you and your glider(s) hang out. Take them out of their cage more often, and give them more pouch time so they feel loved and close to you. When you can't have them out, talk to them as much as possible so they hear your voice. Petting them through the cage can also be a great way to spend just a little extra time with your pet.

Another great option is to offer stimulating toys and a generally interactive environment to try and kill boredom when you're unable to provide attention. Veterinary advice is also a good course of action since they can provide extra advice. If you notice that pacing and back flipping are occurring and/or increasing, seek veterinary care immediately. Both are very serious signs of mental illness and can lead to the death of your sugar glider.

Diarrhea

Diarrhea is something most humans are familiar with, and this includes loose stools, and/or an increase in the amount of stool being passed. Diarrhea can be caused by a viral or bacterial infection, a parasite infection, a bowel disorder, stress, or an intolerance to a specific food.

Signs and symptoms of diarrhea include:
- An increase in bowel movement frequency
- One or more loose, mushy, or runny stools

Treatment for diarrhea includes seeking veterinary care immediately. A veterinarian can determine the cause of the diarrhea so that any treatment given is the most effective in alleviating the issue. In cases of infection, medication may be issued. If the diarrhea is a result of diet, the food causing the problem is eliminated. In both cases, the glider should be given Pedialyte to help prevent dehydration. This can be mixed with their water and put in their water bottle; and it can be offered in a dish throughout the day.

Sugar Glider Readiness Check List

Here are some resources to help in raising your sugar glider.

1) A Cage:
- Cage needs to be fully ventilated (metal cages work better than plastic for this).
- Minimum of 36 x 24 x 36 inches in size for one glider, or a pair of gliders. Larger cages are welcome, but cage should absolutely be no smaller.
- Holes in cage surface should not be large enough to fit the glider's head of body out for safety reasons.

2) Nesting Boxes:
- Several boxes placed/hanging throughout the cage for nesting purposes. Be sure there are enough for all sugar gliders present. 3-4 nesting boxes for a pair is sufficient.

3) Sleeping Pouches:
- 2 – 3 sleeping pouches for a pair of sugar gliders.

4) Bonding Pouch:
- A wearable pouch to carry around your sugar glider in. This provides bonding time, and is especially important when caring for baby sugar gliders.

5) Nail Clippers:
- Small clippers that allow for precision. Baby nail clippers work well, as do small rabbit claw clippers.

6) Hanging Food Bowls:
- These should be medium to small in size.

- 2 – 3 bowls placed throughout the cage for a pair of sugar gliders.

7) Hanging Water Bottles for Small Mammals:
- Small water bottles that encourage frequent changing and refills. Small bottles also have a smaller ball that regulates water flow, thus releasing the right amount for the sugar glider's size, and reducing leakage.
- 2 – 3 bottles placed throughout the cage for a pair of sugar gliders.

8) Cage Bedding:
- Bedding should be placed at the bottom of the cage and in nesting boxes for comfort.
- Bedding can be purchased at a local pet store, or can be made from recycled materials at home. Suggestions for bedding include: aspen shavings (wood shavings), unbleached paper towels (shredded or ripped into smaller pieces), shredded paper (preferably without a lot of ink on it).

9) Exercise Wheels:
- Should have a solid floor, so plastic wheels work well.
- Small in size like a hamster wheel.

10) Healthy Sugar Glider Food:
- Sugar glider food can be made at home regularly using a healthy sugar glider food recipe. This is the best option since sugar gliders have very specific feeding needs.
- A homemade diet can be supplemented with a store bought one, but a store bought diet should not be the only source of nutrition. A homemade diet is best.
- Sugar gliders should have access to fresh fruits and vegetables in their diet.

11) Vitamin Supplements:
- Vitamins and minerals can be put into sugar glider food, or given separately.

- Multi-vitamins can be purchased from local pet stores or through an exotic pet veterinarian.

- Vitamins should contain calcium, but be free of phosphorus.

-Multi-vitamins for cats, dogs, and/or reptiles generally work well for sugar gliders.

12) Transportation Device:
- Sugar gliders will need a safe pet carrier. Soft or hard cat carriers work well.

Quick Tips For Diet And Feeding

- Always add the vitamins to the food supply (sprinkling on fresh fruits and vegetables is optimal), not to the water supply. This ensures that the vitamins get eaten and you can track it. It also ensures that the vitamins don't build up in the water and/or get tossed out when you clean the water. Essentially, you are not able to track whether your sugar glider is getting the vitamins or not, and how much they are or aren't getting, when it is in the water.

- Non-breeding sugar gliders should have a diet consisting 40% protein. More is OK, but they should be served no less. Breeding gliders need a minimum of 50% protein in their diet.

- Never feed your sugar glider cat food as their grazing food or their main entrée. Cat food does not contain the essential dietary elements needed for a healthy, happy sugar glider.

- Feeding your sugar glider in the evening is best as this is when they generally wake up. This also allows them to eat while they are awake, and for you to remove all uneaten food when you wake up in the morning. This will prevent your gliders from eating old and possibly spoiled foods.

- Gut load all insects before feeding them to your gliders in order to provide the highest nutritional value.

- Avoid providing any foods with preservatives to your sugar glider. Fresh fruits and vegetables are best. If you're unable to provide fresh fruits and vegetables, freeze them and thaw before serving.

- Treat sugar gliders only after they have eaten their primary meal (or at least a significant portion of it). This is done in order to ensure that your glider gets those foods that provide the nutrition that is so essential to their survival, and to ensure that they do not feed on too many treats and become obese.

Foods That Are Unsafe For Your Pet

While there are a wide variety of foods that sugar gliders can enjoy, there are also some that are considered unsafe for sugar glider consumption, and should be avoided at all costs. These foods are believed to cause serious problems and illness in sugar gliders.

- Garlic (or anything with garlic in it, such as baby foods containing garlic)
- Coffee
- Raw eggs
- Onions (or anything with onions in it, such as baby foods containing onion)
- Leeks
- Milk
- Canned foods (including canned fruits and vegetables. If you cannot buy fresh fruits and vegetables, purchase frozen)
- Chives
- Raisins
- Peanuts
- Tea
- Wild insects (insects not raised as food for pets can carry diseases that may transmit to your sugar glider)
- Chocolate
- Millet
- Fried foods (including fried snacks like potato chips)
- Soda
- Raw meat products
- Scallions
- Sugar
-Processed meats (like hot dogs)
-Rhubarb

Sugar Glider Safe Foods

There are a number of sugar glider safe food options, and this is by no means an exhaustive list. However, it is a greater resource for safe food ideas. Of course, use common sense when preparing your pet's diet. If you are unsure about a particular element of the food (such as the skin or seeds) err on the side of caution and remove them. Similarly, wash all fresh produce thoroughly before serving to eliminate pesticides.

Fruit:
-Blueberries
-Raspberries
-Mulberries
-Orange and Orange Peel
-Mandarin Orange
-Mango
-Tangerine
-Nectarine
-Apples
-Coconut
-Peaches
-Pears
-Currants
-Watermelon
-Avocado
-Cantaloupe
-Lime and Lime Peel
-Lemon and Lemon Peel
-Banana
-Plantain
-Cranberries
-Figs

-Papaya
-Apricot
-Grapefruit
-Kiwi
-Gooseberries
-Pummelo
-Pomegranate
-Tamarind
-Guava
-Honeydew Melon
-Dates
-Tomato
-Plum
-Cherries
-Strawberries
-Passion Fruit
-Loquats
-Kumquats
-Pineapple
-Cherimoya

Vegetables:
-Lettuce (Iceberg, Butterhead, leaf lettuce in dark green, Romaine)
-Cabbage
-Endive
-Celery
-Artichoke
-Turnip
-Green Beans
-Lima Beans
-Soy Beans
-Potatoes
-Yams
-Zucchini
-Broccoli
-Cauliflower

-Peas
-Snow Peas
-Okra
-Burdock Root
-Cucumber
-Kale
-Ginger (Root)
-Beets
-Kohlrabi
-Corn
-Jicama
-Carrots
-Spinach
-Eggplant
-Green Pepper
-Red Pepper
-Asparagus
-Pumpkin
-Squash (Acorn, Summer, Winter, Spaghetti)

Quick Bonding Tips

Because bonding with your sugar glider is such a big deal, here are some quick tips on how to improve the relationship between you and your sugar glider.

- Buy a pouch or purse you're comfortable taking along with you everywhere. Your sugar glider likes traveling with you, and many owners like to take their sugar gliders out on errands with them. As long as your glider is safe, this is a great way to make them feel comfortable and loved, as well as stave off mental illnesses like depression.

- Keep your sugar glider cage in the room where you spend the most time during your wakeful hours. While having your gliders in your bedroom may be difficult because they are up most of the night, if you spend much of your time there, it is the best option. Leaving your sugar glider(s) alone too much is not recommended as they can easily become depressed and lonely. Having the cage in a room where you spend a great deal of time allows you to interact with your sugar gliders even when you don't have them out. You can talk to them and pet them as you move around the room.

- Offer treats as incentives for interaction when you're getting to know your glider. Treats are also a great way to show your glider love throughout the day.

Conclusion

Sugar Gliders can make great pets for the right people. Please make sure you are ready for the responsibility. Think of it as adding a child to your home. Asugar glider will take a lot of time, love and care, but they will also give you much enjoyment and love in return.

Product References

1) High protein wombaroo powder:
http://store.sweet-sugar-gliders.com/HPW-High-Protein-Wombaroo.html

2) Australian bee pollen:
a) http://store.sweet-sugar-gliders.com/Australian-Bee-Pollen.html
b) http://www.beepollen.com.au/
c) http://www.bee-pollen-buzz.com/bee-pollen-products-cart.html

3) Gliderade:
http://store.sweet-sugar-gliders.com/Gliderade.html

4) Rep-Cal Calcium:
http://www.sugar-gliders.com/rep-cal-calcium.htm

5) Vionate Vitamin and Mineral Supplement:
http://www.sugar-gliders.com/vionate.htm

6) ZooKeeper's Secret:
http://www.sugar-gliders.com/zookeepers-secret.htm

7) Wholesome Balance Chicken and Brown Rice Blend:

http://www.sugar-gliders.com/wholesome-balance.htm

8) Gut Load Cricket and Insect Food:

http://www.sugar-gliders.com/gut-load.htm

RECIPE REFERENCES

(1) Sweet Sugar Gliders (2009). Sugar Glider HPW Diet – High Protein Wombaroo Recipe.
   http://www.sweet-sugar-gliders.com/sugar-glider-hpw-diet-high-protein-wombaroo-recipe.html

(2) Sweet Sugar Gliders (2009). Suncoast Diet Recipe.
   http://www.sweet-sugar-gliders.com/suncoast-diet-recipe.html

(3) Sweet Sugar Gliders (2009). Judie's BML Recipe – A Sugar Glider Modified BML Diet.
   http://www.sweet-sugar-gliders.com/judies-bml-recipe.html

About The Author

David Oconner has been writing and publishing books on many of his varied interests. He has books on topics such as Cichlid Fish, How to Grow Tomatoes, Sugar Gliders, How to Play Minecraft, Diablo III and more.

###

Made in the USA
Lexington, KY
26 January 2015